I Paint Blu

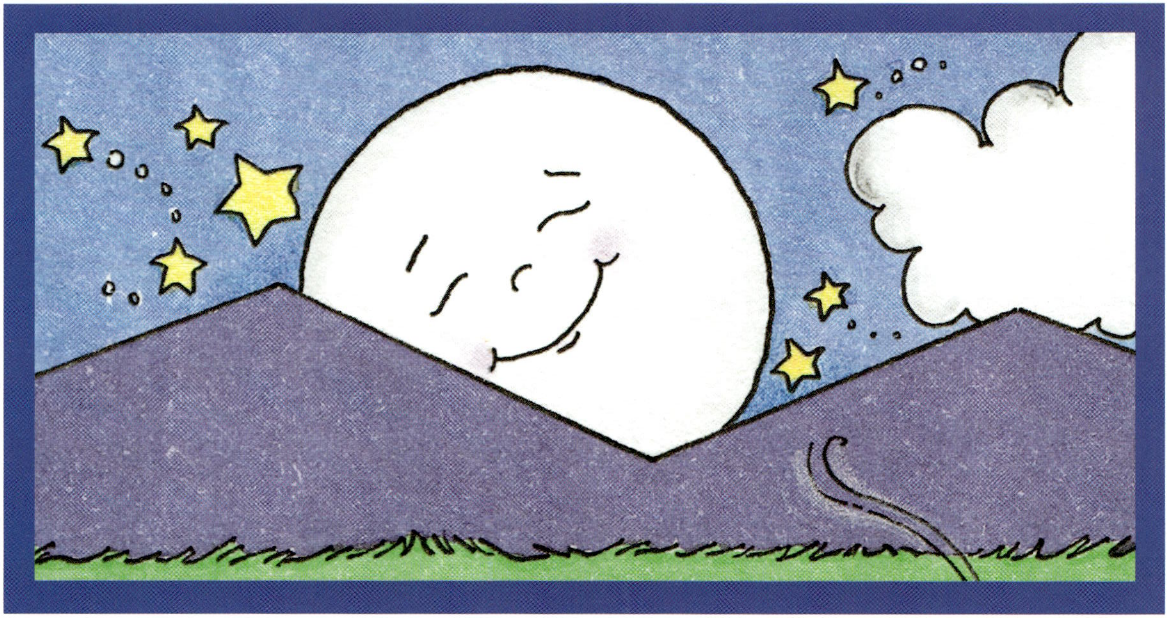

Rockin' Readers: I Paint Blue

Illustrated by Sharon Holm
Project Director: Carolea Williams
Editor: Carla Hamaguchi
Art Director: Tom Cochrane
Designer: Carmela Murray

Published in the United States of America by:
Creative Teaching Press, Inc.
P.O. Box 2723
Huntington Beach, CA 92647-0723

ISBN: 1-57471-763-4
CTP 2766

I paint blue, ocean and sky.

I paint green, leaves on trees.

I paint yellow daffodils.

I paint red, red roses.

I paint purple, violet mountains.

I paint summer, sunshine too.

I paint winter, spring, and fall.
I paint white, then green and golden.

I paint sun, golden yellow.

I paint moon, full and white.

I paint you, I paint me,
Arm in arm, happy and free.

I paint a rainbow of faces from near and far places—
friends, neighbors and family,
For a picnic in a park, in a place called planet earth,
planet home, planet me.

I paint blue, dolphins diving.

I paint green, emerald forest.

I paint wishes.
I paint dreams.

Don’t you like my picture?